Coffee Quiet

Coffee Quiet

Poems by

Jeffrey Johannes

Cover image by Firdaus Ramadhan
Cover design by Shay Culligan
Author photo by Dave Engel

ISBN: 978-1-63980-476-4

Kelsay Books
502 South 1040 East, A-119
American Fork, Utah 84003
Kelsaybooks.com

For Joan

In winter woods
I cup
your breath
whisper words
on frosted neck
sculpt
a wind sonnet
tender and profane.

Acknowledgments

Thank you to the following publications in which versions of these poems previously appeared:

Ariel Anthology: "Braille Reader," "Puget Sound"
The Aurorean: "For Becca," previously published as
    "For Kimberly"
The Best of Kindness Origami Poems 2016 Anthology:
    "Faith in Us"
Bramble: "Accept the Miracles," "Between Waking and Sleep,"
    "The Beauty of Physics," "My Neighbor Wanders into
    My Dream," "Contemplation IV"
Fox Cry Review: "Sent to Our Rooms"
Lockdown 2020: "Contemplation III," "Searching for a Spell"
Moss Piglet: "If Truth Be Told"
Norbert Blei's Poetry Dispatch: "Some Winter Day"
Poetry Jumps Off the Shelf: "Luna Moth"
Portage Magazine: "Contemplation I"
Red Cedar Review: "In the Peeling Paint"
Peninsula Pulse: "My Wife Looks at Art," "Grace"
Sheltering with Poems: Community & Connection:
    "Contemplation V"
Soundings: Door County in Poetry: "Sleeping in the Cliff House"
Stoneboat: "Paws Folded"
Verse Virtual: "Because of the War"
Wisconsin Poets' Calendar: "True Blue," "Romance,"
    "Cold Spell"
Wisconsin Fellowship of Poets 65th Anniversary Quilt: "An
    Ambulance Stops by the Park"
World Enough Writers Coffee Anthology: "Silence," "Visitation"

I am grateful for the valuable input from The Entendres, Mid-State Poetry Towers, and Riverwood Round Table; and to Marilyn Taylor for her encouragement, insightful critique, and blurb, as well as to Robin Chapman and John Bloner for their thoughtful words. Of course, I also want to thank Joan Wiese Johannes, my love and companion in all things creative in this world and the next.

Contents

Silence	11
Luna Moth	12
Faith in Us	13
In the Peeling Paint	14
Sent to Our Rooms	15
My Wife Looks at Art	16
How Can You Sleep?	17
Romance	18
Sleeping in the Cliff House	19
My Neighbor Wanders into My Dream	20
True Blue	21
Visitation	22
Contemplation I	23
Contemplation II	24
Contemplation III	25
Contemplation IV	26
Contemplation V	27
Some Winter Day	28
Blue	29
An Ambulance Stops by the Park	30
Grace	31
Because of the War	32
Searching for a Spell	33
Braille Reader	34
Puget Sound	35
Accept the Miracles	36
Paws Folded	37
If Truth Be Told	38
Between Waking and Sleep	39
The Beauty of Physics	40
Blessings of Light	41
Cold Spell	42
The Last Poet	43

Silence

Sometimes fog
surrounds morning
in a white room;
then the silence
of sunlight seeps
into balsam shadows.
Steam is silence too,
slipping over the brim
of bone china
in the coffee-quiet
of morning.

Luna Moth

for Edith Nash

Something calls me
to the garage
where she sleeps
heavy in sun,
upside down,
an oriental kite
napping on the rim
of the moon.
A hickory breeze
brushes her dreams
with the promise
of star nectar.

Faith in Us

Sometimes I choose
a spot on a quiet page
and write down
something unusual
such as the story
of how everyone
on a street
in Chinatown
walked carefully
while a woman chased
hundreds of tiny turtles
after they got loose
from a tank
in her market stall.
Not one turtle
was harmed.
And this mercy
lifts my spirits,
reminds me that
acts of kindness
appear like moths
circling our porch lights,
drawn to the light.

In the Peeling Paint

For a moment I see the face
of a swan as the face
of a saint or messiah—
white plumes
a black bill
but no halo.
And although
I would not kneel
before a poet or priest,
I would kneel before a swan,
its wings meeting
like folded hands,
the curve of its neck
a cathedral arch.

Sent to Our Rooms

The whole world
should be sent
to their rooms
while Earth
sighs with relief,
leans back,
closes weary eyes,
and soaks
her bruised feet
in glacial lakes.
For one blessed day,
let the sun warm
her millions
of wounded miles;
let the moon caress
her millions of scars.

My Wife Looks at Art

I find her by a watercolor
dazzled by the brightness of koi
the way a child is drawn to fire.

But this is nothing new.

Once she stood on my shoulders
to climb onto the porch roof
and reached toward the night sky
in a way Rousseau might have posed
a maiden under an endless
ribbon of rainbows.

When I joined her, we lay together
and counted the spaces between
clouds where moonlight fell,
our bodies like small boats unmoored
and adrift, lost in the looking.

How Can You Sleep?

Yielding to sleep,
you dream of the poem
you may write
tomorrow while I
follow a path
along the shore
and cast a Hula Popper
into the stillness
of Sissabagama.
Across the bay
tremolos and wails
herald the hatching
of a chick.
My heart is
timber wolf wild
in cadence
with their ballyhoo,
their laughter,
their bright looning.

Romance

I will not tell you the whole story
of how dawn begins her journey
in the heart of a white pony
somewhere in the field of night
when the world is lit
by only a few, cold stars
or the reason why she gallops
through my window every morning,
but I will confess to the warmth
that moves inside me whenever
she nuzzles my hand as if to
convince me to rub her ears
or to remind me to look under
my pillow for the sugar I may
have forgotten to give her yesterday.

Sleeping in the Cliff House

Drumming echoes through cedar
Evening's softness spreads
My palms open like a clam shell
Across the bay, thunderheads purl

Evening's softness spreads
Seagulls fly white over raven water
Across the bay, thunderheads purl
The open window frames the moon

Seagulls fly white over raven water
Somewhere the barred owl waits
The open window frames the moon
Candlelight is the color of butter

Somewhere the barred owl waits
My palms open like a clam shell
Candlelight is the color of butter
Drumming echoes through cedar

My Neighbor Wanders into My Dream

When my neighbor naps in his yard,
a blue-eyed darner lights on his brow,
its lacy wings open and jeweled body
a dream-pole pointing toward the sun.
A smile shapes the corners of his mouth
as my dream becomes his dream,
becomes our dream.

He loves sharing the dreams in which
my wife is a cloudless sky echoing
with the wingbeats of wild geese
or in which he is standing by a window
watching her hang laundry,
her bare shoulders tan like an island girl
in a painting by Gauguin.

He doesn't understand why a wren
is chasing my wife's ring finger,
flitting from clothespin to clothespin,
but I know dreams are only dreams.
I forgive him.

True Blue

In the aftermath
of the storm,
I am struck by the iamb
of its passage
that could have been
measured in a heartbeat

and by the ease
with which trees descended
on a sleeping landscape,
a green tsunami
leafed in maple and oak

and by the way
an indigo bunting,
still damp,
lies in my garden
without drama,
only the fade of its blue.

Visitation

for Monet

He strolls through
my second cup
of coffee,
a cathedral seeking
sunlight and hay,
paint splatter
accenting his beard.
He gavottes
across blue tile,
a water lily dancing
out my sunroom door.

Contemplation I

What is it like to grow old?

Each day
must be wrestled
for its beauty,
enjoyed
for the dizziness
of a glass of wine
with someone
you love;
and when you sleep
lightly, turning
your body
side to side,
you must relax
and listen
to the coyotes'
yips and cries
to the million
passing moments
and the distant
sound of a train.

Contemplation II

Who do I want to visit me?

I am saving the guest
room for a small god
who plays the lyre
in a way that melts hearts
and extracts wisdom
teeth without pain.
We will sit
on the porch drinking
Orange Crush.
She will explain
why street lights
sometimes wear halos
and the moon is
both cold and warm.

Contemplation III

Why do I feel dread?

It is good to say,
"Good night"
as each day ends.
What lies ahead may
be an empty field
in which all of us
are laid out like cards
face down
in a losing game
of solitaire.
The night sky
will fill with stars
even if the lights
go out one by one.
The white deer
that roams
behind my house
will still glow
in moonlight.

Contemplation IV

How much does Death weigh?

Two crows fly
across the field
to peck insects among
the ripening tomatoes,
and I am once
again reminded
of dwindling years.
One day I will no longer
sing or dance
or write a poem
about one crow
vanishing
beyond the lilacs
and the other rising
in a slow way
over yellow coneflowers,
the weight of a chipmunk
in its beak.

Contemplation V

for Bryan Alft

What is the news tonight?

Last night my friend
in Minneapolis sat
on a lawn chair
in his yard drinking tea;
it was his turn to watch
over the neighborhood
in the wild darkness.
Ash in the wind,
flames just blocks away,
the voices of crickets.

Some Winter Day

Think of winter as the creative
recluse who emerges
from his half of your duplex
to borrow a cup of sugar.
He sits at your table sipping coffee,
frost clinging to his beard.
Your coffee still too hot to drink,
conversation drifts.
You try to remind him about color:
daffodils, playground chalk, koi—
but he only wants to talk
about his latest composition,
an opera in which the protagonist
paints the world white.
It takes him all morning to sing
the opening aria.
Outside your window
snow lifts and curls.
You light a cigarette,
pour some Irish whiskey
into your coffee,
and settle in for the second act.

Blue

The modest role played by blue in ancient societies and the difficulties many ancient languages have in even naming it caused many nineteenth-century researchers to wonder if the men and women of antiquity could see the color blue.
—Michel Pastoureau, *Blue: The History of a Color*

We know it never brightened dark Lascaux
in torchlight dim on ancient limestone wall.
The freehand ease of bison and of doe
were never blue phantasmagorical.
No blue in poems in gray medieval France;
no story of Blue Riding Hood was told
when blue was hidden waiting for our glance.
While blue filled up our world with pigment bold
as bluebirds melted into clear blue sky,
no people paid attention to the hue.
What unsung role did blue exemplify
before its recognition overdue?
Yet, now the sight of blue brings no surprise:
blue jeans, blue jays, blue moon, blue mood, your eyes.

An Ambulance Stops by the Park

My neighbors look
like lawn ornaments,
some talking softly,
others just staring.
Children on bikes
circle flashing lights.
And finally, a boy
on inline skates
glides backwards
telling each gawker
what has happened
in the park;
he pirouettes
with self importance.

Grace

for Dave Cervenka

I loved you most for the kindness
you showed the ground bees in your garden,
the way you bent and pulled up thistle

from your berry patch after a rain,
your sweaty, tee-shirt stretched
across the horizon of your belly.

You told me stories of your father's farm,
the slope of land in the south field,
swallows lifting above the round barn,

how your mother took vegetables
to the market each Saturday in summer.
The earth is generous, and so were you,

the neighbor who came to a neighbor's
door offering gifts from his garden—
beans, carrots, sugar snap peas.

Only last week at the village picnic,
I watched the children buzz
around the hive of your generosity.

Two days later you collapsed,
a glory of vegetables falling
from your arms, your heart still open.

Because of the War

In the box in the attic
I find the folded fan
my father bought in Japan
and think of young women
eye lashes fluttering
like black butterflies
above pale faces.
Rice paper unfolds
on sticks
and cranes unpleat
white as pear blossoms
their crests
like curved red lips.

Searching for a Spell

An amulet touched
while giving voice
to curing words
clears a path
where thorns
are too thick to pass,
and ashes of a barn
swallow, mixed
with honey,
soothe ailing eyes
while a charm
of wild onion,
trillium, and thyme
makes the sun brighter—
if only for a moment.

Braille Reader

You caress my poem,
find its heartbeat
with finger and thumb.
I listen to the pull
of your fingertips
as they slide out
of shadow into sight.
You wade along
the page's shore,
a flash of minnows
circling while you grasp
the black bear gait
of words,
following them
into a patch of berries.
I watch you touch
my poem as you feel
the light and dark.

Puget Sound

for Wayne McCleskey, the facilitator
of the Pacific NW Flute Gathering

On Vashon Island
a harbor seal slices
early light as thin
as a fish-bone needle
in Grandmother's hand,
and flute song floats
over pine and spruce.
The truth is never loud
until Crow,
as if he flew a mile
just to be here,
caws a gratitude
that can't be conveyed
during the silence
between heartbeats.

Accept the Miracles

Two thousand years ago
a prophet spoke in parables,
and on the other side
of the mountain,
blind monks tended
sacred elephants
holding up the universe.

Last spring a doe gave
birth near our pond,
and somewhere a butterfly
is lighting on a coffin
being lowered
into the ground.

There are those among
the faithful who have
seen the face of Allah
in an open avocado,
and once Neruda,
his heart lost in a sonnet,
looked into the eyes
of his dog and saw God.

Paws Folded

Angels are born inside old dogs,
cradled in the chambers of faithful hearts.
They view the world through cloudy eyes
and guide their hosts into cathedrals,
claws clicking on marble floors
as they sniff for the perfect pew
or roll over and doze in rainbows
of stained glass light.
Awash with everlasting joy,
they tilt their heads and listen to nuns
whose prayers soar heavenward
and to sinners kneeling on cold stone,
their way uncertain, world without end.
When choirs sing, and organs swell
those sweeping arcs with thunder,
they fold their paws
and howl to the glory of God.

If Truth Be Told

Miss Muffet weaves her way
from therapist to therapist
admitting how the pale sound
of orb weavers spinning webs

calls to her on warm nights
and that a violin spider
hiding by her patio door
wants to wed her to his bite.

Spiders have always loved her.

Tarantulas wait in the dim light
after sunset, hoping to see her
in the yard filling the bird bath.
Wolf spiders bask on her deck,

and the nursery web spider
on her armoire watches her sleep,
admiring the silk of her hair,
eager to set out in search

of a fly to stir her heart.

Between Waking and Sleep

Before the first bird sings,
I hear morning stir
like the distant notes
of a saxophone,
and my dreams become
Chinese kites
floating in sunlight,
bottle rockets
tattooing night,
the slow explosion
of lichens on rocks,
and the unexpected colors
of ghosts.

The Beauty of Physics

Viewed from the outside, the universe is beige.
—Karl Glazebrook, astronomer

The universe is beige,
not the hospital beige
of a world pulling away
when I am down on my luck
or the mother beige that embraces
an infant who doesn't know
what is in store,
but the ephemeral beige
of cedar waxwings flying,
the quiet beige of
  a sigh
  a swoon
  a misty moon
  a soft cotton dress
  an old soft-shoe—
beige the color of pebbles
tossed gently at your window.

Blessings of Light

It's a photograph!
　—Ansel Adams

Between the raven and the swan
there is grayness,
a place where the moon shines
on bioluminous squid,
their shared light merging
in shallow water.
Downtown, long arcs of neon
flash a secret code in gas and light
while somewhere a child connects
time and space.
The mind always wants more,
which is why I reflect on light,
its glow lingering in evening sky
with nothing more than some
dim notion of the infinite left
in its wake,
and why I always look closely
at *Moonrise, Hernandez, NM, 1941*
knowing the world held its breath
in the round eye of his lens,
a sacred place where light
gathered and bent in beatitudes
of black, white, and gray.

Cold Spell

All it takes is a dream
to catch me by surprise—

a lover from my past
standing at the foot
of my bed,
a glass of Merlot
in her hand.

I toss back the blanket,
walk to the kitchen
cradling the cat
as I look out the window.

Moonlight settles
on the frozen field

where a gentle snow filled
this emptiness last night;
a doe lifts her head
and listens when I say,

You   are beautiful.

The Last Poet

This morning I breathe the deep scent
of coffee and wonder where
I read that every cup equals

one dead songbird somewhere.
Their songs fade with every sip;
bright plumage scatters and mats

like the tug of heartache in a poem.
I think about poets as birds moving
from one coffee house to another

smug in the echo and throb, fledging
forward as they peep their hoot and caw,
the audience lost in the forest

of small talk and steaming mugs.
Then unexpectedly one poet takes wing
in a bright blue haiku,

syllables and feathers soaring
while the coffee grows cold.
Some morning when it is too cold to hunt

for poems and too cold for the poems
to move about making themselves known,
the last poet will cross a furrowed field,

hands clasped around a cup of coffee,
with each sip thinking nothing's forever,
fear and desire on well-versed lips.

About the Author

Jeffrey Johannes is a life-long resident of Wisconsin and has been publishing poetry for over twenty-five years. His poem, "My Wife Looks at Art," won the Hal Prize from *Peninsula Pulse;* "Grace" earned Honorable Mention; "Faith in Us" placed second in the Origami Poems Project's Kindness Contest; "Paws Folded" received Honorable Mention from *Presence: An International Journal of Spiritual Direction;* and "An Ambulance Stops by the Park" was third in the Wisconsin Fellowship of Poets 65th Anniversary Poetry Quilt Contest.

Jeffrey's poems, including "The Last Poet," have placed in other contests and/or been published in journals and anthologies, including *Allegro & Adagio: Dance Poems II, Celestial Musings: Poems Inspired by the Night Sky, English Journal, Milwaukee Journal Sentinel, Modern Haiku, Nimrod,* and *Rosebud.*

Also a visual artist, Jeffrey's art is in the permanent collections of the University of Wisconsin Stevens Point, Charles A. Wustum Museum of Fine Arts in Racine, WI, and Wheaton College, Norton MA; and has been displayed throughout the midwest and won various awards. Jeffrey also creates cartoons of his more humorous poems, which he calls "pometoons." After teaching art for thirty-four years at Lincoln High School in Wisconsin Rapids where he was Teacher of the Year and a recipient of a Kohl Fellowship, he enjoys retirement in Port Edwards with his poet wife Joan and their fourteen-year-old golden retriever Sophie.

www.ingramcontent.com/pod-product-compliance
Lightning Source LLC
Chambersburg PA
CBHW030815090426
42737CB00010B/1284